T0159595

ALMOST HAPPY

ALMOST HAPPY

PUSHING YOUR BUTTONS
WITH REVERSE PSYCHOLOGY

DR. BRIAN KAPLAN
and HEPHZIBAH KAPLAN

Loba Publishing
Charleston, SC

Almost Happy

This book is not intended as a substitute for the medical advice of physicians.
The reader should regularly consult a physician in matters relating to his/her
health and particularly with respect to any symptoms that may require diagnosis
or medical attention.

First Edition
Printed in China

eBook ISBN: 978-1-952019-35-7
Paperback ISBN: 978-1-952019-35-7

For Jonah

Life is far too important a thing ever to
talk seriously about it.
—Oscar Wilde, *Lady Windermere's Fan*

Against the assault of laughter, nothing can stand.
—Mark Twain, *The Mysterious Stranger*

FRIENDLY WARNING

Please do not read this book if you don't have a sense
of humor about issues in your personal life or are more
likely to be offended than amused.

CONTENTS

INTRODUCTION

Laughter is the best medicine—or so they say—but as a practicing doctor, I can assure you it isn't always true. There are much better treatments for appendicitis, cardiac arrest, fractured bones and thousands of other medical conditions. Still, laughter is more than just an excellent general tonic; it has actually been proven to be good for our physical health in many ways.[1]

Inspired by the work of the famous doctor and clown Patch Adams, I composed this mnemonic many years ago to collate the evidence-based health benefits of laughter:

1   Starting in the 1960s, Dr. William F. Fry spent decades at Stanford University documenting the proven health benefits of laughter and has deservedly been dubbed the "grandfather of gelotology" — the scientific study of laughter.

SMILEE

S STRESS hormones: Epinephrine, norepinephrine, and cortisol are reduced.

M MUSCULAR relaxation: Muscles take two hours to return to previous state of tension after a big belly laugh.

I IMMUNITY: Increased antibodies in blood after laughter improves resistance to colds and other infections.

L LUNGS are helped by laughter expelling stale air, allowing more fresh air to enter.

E EXERCISE: One hundred belly laughs a day give you as much beneficial exercise as ten minutes of rowing—and without the agonized expression that rowers, stationary cyclists, and joggers customarily have on their faces.

E ENDORPHINS and ENCEPHALONS: Natural high-making chemicals of the body are increased by laughter.

Laughter has also been shown to be good for our hearts and in 2015 the *Journal of Psychosomatic Medicine* published a Norwegian paper demonstrating a clear link between having a sense of humor and living longer.[2] Who knows how many more physical benefits will eventually be discovered for laughter?

2 Solfrid Romundstad, Sven Svebak, Are Holen, and Jostein Holmen. "A 15-Year Follow-Up Study Of Sense Of Humor And Causes Of Mortality," *Psychosomatic Medicine* 78 no. 3 (2016): 345–353.

Laughter is beneficial for our mental health too. As lifelong fans of all forms of comedy, we have seen over and over how laughter can have a profound effect on our well-being. We are happier and more at ease when we are laughing. While we would not claim spiritual benefits for laughter, many gurus and charismatic religious leaders are known for chuckling away while sharing their wisdom.

If laughter is good for us holistically—body, mind, and spirit—then it may just be the ideal psycho-physiological state in which to face the uncomfortable challenge of dealing with our personal difficulties. Actually this process is happening all the time. Many therapeutic conversations are taking place right now between family members and friends who genuinely care for each other. If we could listen in on these heart-to-hearts we would not be surprised to find these healing conversations enriched by jokes, humor, and laughter—even though the subject matter may be serious. It's the way most of us are made. We find it easier to face painful truths about ourselves while we are being comforted by the healing effects of laughter.

Wouldn't it be refreshing if there were a therapeutic approach that used laughter and comedy to help us, not only to feel better, but to provoke us to discover, own, and enact authentic solutions to many of our issues?

Well the good news is that there is indeed such an approach. It's called *Provocative Therapy*,[3] and it's one of the inspirations behind this book. It was developed in the1960s by an innovative therapist named Frank Farrelly of Madison, Wisconsin. Frank, our teacher and mentor, stumbled on the idea while trying to help a patient whose sense of hopelessness hadn't responded to anything he had tried in over ninety sessions of therapy. Finally Farrelly decided to try something different; he *agreed* with the patient that there was indeed *no solution to his problem.* The response of the patient was electric: "What do you mean? There *has* to be a solution!" And the first tool of Provocative Therapy was born: *There is no solution to your problem.* The patient went on to enjoy a complete recovery, and many other provocative tools were subsequently developed by Frank, others and ourselves. (See Appendix III).

Almost Happy is influenced by three core principles central to Provocative Therapy:

I) Reverse psychology, a powerful psychological technique known to almost every parent, also works on adults.

II) People don't like being told what to do. That's why if you cheerfully make a case for them to continue the behavior that is keeping them unhappy or only almost happy, they often start to prescribe sensible solutions for themselves.

---

3   Frank Farrelly and Jeff Brandsma. *Provocative Therapy*. Cupertino, CA: Meta publ., 1974.

Because they own those solutions, they are more likely to implement them.

III) Irony, satire, and parody can be used warmly to provoke the emergence of the voice of conscience and common sense.

When using reverse psychology in the clinic to help people change, it has to be clear to the client that the therapist or coach is employing a gentle form of teasing, the objective of which is genuine and heartfelt. It is also vital for the client to give permission for humor and reverse psychology to be used in this way. Nobody should ever be ambushed by this contrarian approach, which is why we ask people to give explicit, verbal permission for the process before using it in therapy and in our *Almost Happy* workshops.

Now we need to ask *your* permission: Are you ready to read a book that will tease you about some of your issues? If not, stop reading now! Or are you prepared to take a chance and accept that the buttons and provocative suggestions in this book are offered to you with a twinkle in the eye and affection in the heart?

If so—read on!

The *Almost Happy* buttons were developed over twenty years of clinical practice and running *Almost Happy* workshops for the general public and health professionals. While exploring obstacles and blocks to happiness—via creative therapeutic processes such as improvisation, humor, and art-making—we started to personify these obstructive behavioral patterns and found nicknames to label them.

Once we began identifying these disruptive "voices", far from being insulted, people enjoyed having the annoying parts of themselves comically labeled in this way. We bought a button maker and started designing buttons for individual people. At our *Almost Happy* workshops, the buttons became a major part of the process but were never imposed on participants. We simply showed people a selection of buttons we thought might suit them and invited them to choose one. Everyone seemed delighted to discover buttons for their annoying subselves (or subpersonalities) and were keen to take their buttons home at the end of the workshop. But what are these subselves or subpersonalities?

It is clear to most of us that we are not one person with one consistent personality. We are composed of several subselves such as the inner child, teenage rebel, drama queen, control freak, and many others. This is not a new theory. Dozens of eminent psychologists agree on the existence of various subselves (also referred to as sub-personalities, archetypes, or I-positions—see Appendix IV). The pioneering work of Hal and Sidra Stone[4] and John Rowan[5] were particularly influential in our appreciation of the importance of our subselves and how they influence our behavior.

In our work, we noticed time and again the sabotaging voices of domineering subselves in patients and clients. When our sub-selves are working well together, we feel balanced and contented. Unfortunately we don't always stay in balance and it's very common for one of our subselves to grab the megaphone, become dictatorial, and start dominating the others. We start to feel unhinged and un-happy as our inner orchestra of subselves loses its harmony. Friends and family get used to Sarah acting bossy, Rob being grumpy, Bill demanding attention, and Patti throwing a tantrum. These are sim-ple examples of where a subself can become dominant in a person and change their behavior—often for the worse. We are all capable of slipping into mindsets that do not serve us well. Fortunately there are ways to put an overbearing subself back in its box.

Almost Happy uses a radical approach to soften the effects of a domineering subself. The buttons are designed as comic mirrors to lampoon our overbearing subselves—and by laughing at them decrease their power over us. In the design of the buttons and accompanying text, we use humor, irony, and satire to quieten

4   Stone, Hal, and Sidra Stone. 2011. *Embracing Our Selves.* [United States]: New World Library.
5   Rowan, John. 2017. *Discover Your Subpersonalities.* Routledge.

and disempower the parts of you that have become too loud. When we are unaware that a powerful subself has taken control of us, it has immense power. By using the buttons to become playfully aware of our dominating subselves, we lessen the grip they have on our lives. It has long been advocated that it is healthy to laugh at yourself. *Almost Happy* buttons are never aimed at your essential Self, only at those irritating subselves that are holding you back.

Mark Twain's maxim "Against the assault of laughter, nothing can stand"[6] is a perfect maxim for the *Almost Happy* approach; once you get your inner joke in this way, change becomes possible. If a few of these buttons can get you to laugh or smile at the parts of yourself that can become dominant and unbalance you, those parts of you *will* start to become quieter.

Readers of *Almost Happy* generally find several buttons that suit different aspects of themselves. You are often aware of which parts are too dominant and are candidates for being disempowered by humor and reverse psychology. When you find one of your buttons, you may laugh, smile, or even get a slight shock. An experience like this is valuable, as it can give you a jolt and provoke a meaningful inner conversation with the disruptive subself. Laughing at the part of yourself that is causing you difficulty can often be liberating, enlightening, and fun!

6   Twain, Mark. 1916. *The Mysterious Stranger*. New York: Harper & Bros.

While it can also be amusing to recognize buttons that comically mirror potent subselves of family, friends, colleagues, and people in the news, it is vital to remember that each button is aimed not at any whole person, only at a commonly occurring subself that may be sabotaging his or her life and relationships. That doesn't always make their behavior forgivable, but it does help us understand it better. The way that a subself has been allowed to dominate a person can elicit both laughter and compassion. We recommend that you read *Almost Happy* with compassion for yourself and everyone else.

Finally, the process works perfectly when *you* choose the buttons that you instinctively know suit your own troublesome subselves. Then you can browse through the *Provocative Suggestions* offered and see if any of them provoke you with reverse psychology to soften the undermining voice of that particular subself.

When you select an *Almost Happy* button for yourself, you can be certain that you are not alone in doing so. Every button suits millions of other people held back by the subself it satirizes. When you laugh at your personal collection of buttons, know that you are sharing a joke with thousands of similar people from the past, present and future. Laughing at your personal inner joke in this way can provoke the emergence of a more congruent and happier you.

THE KEY TO READING *ALMOST HAPPY*

You don't actually have to read *Almost Happy* to get something out of it!

You can just flip through the buttons until you smile, laugh, or find yourself staring blankly at the page. One of your buttons may have been pushed, giving you the chance to be amused at an aspect of yourself that is holding you back. Whether you recognize a button that suits you or someone you know, it is essential to remember to be compassionate toward yourself as well as others.

WHO IS THIS BUTTON FOR?

Here we have nicknames, satirical labels, or slang terms for the subself or aspect of self, for whom the button on the opposite page is a comic mirror.

Note that none of these terms refers to a whole person—only to those parts of us that have become too loud and dominant for our own good.

PROVOCATIVE SUGGESTIONS

The tongue-in-cheek "advice" offered here uses reverse psychology, irreverence, and irony to provoke you to quieten those willful subselves that need to be challenged.

Not every suggestion or "sujestion" will suit the loud personal subself you have identified. Just one having the desired provocative effect should do the trick.

These provocative suggestions ultimately aim to provoke in all of us the emergence of the voice of common sense and conscience.

FOOTNOTES

These comprise references and explanations (both serious and satirical) of psychobabble and technical terms. They may also provide useful information and occasionally refer to further reading.

CHAPTER 1: BAD HABITS

We humans are creatures of habit, which means most of us also have a few habits that are harmful. Some bad habits damage your health, others jeopardize your work or income, and others undermine important relationships in your life. You know your bad habits well and would probably like to dump them. Perhaps you believe you would be happy *if only* you could kick one or two habits that are holding you back and preventing you from leading a more fulfilling life.

In this chapter you will find buttons that make fun of many unhealthy habits and addictions that are common today. When you recognize a button that is mocking one of your habits, know that the button is aimed only at the *part of you* that has become overbearing and keeps insisting that you perpetuate the habit. No button or provocative suggestion is ever aimed at you or anyone else as a whole person—only at the subself that is hooked on the bad habit. Laughing, or even just smiling, at this unhelpfully compulsive part of yourself can loosen its influence over you.

WHO IS THIS BUTTON FOR?

Procrastinators.

Those who detest the word "now."

Anyone thinking of changing their behavior after reading this.

PROVOCATIVE SUGGESTIONS

Never underestimate the Power of Tomorrow!

Always make magnanimous resolutions on your finest night, New Year's Eve.

Meditate on the many horrible consequences of most impulsive decisions and actions.

Return to this page at a later date.

WHO IS THIS BUTTON FOR?

Smokers dying to quit.

Anyone tired of lurking outside for a nicotine fix.

PROVOCATIVE SUGGESTIONS

Enjoy tobacco without guilt—if you know you can't quit, why further damage your health with negative emotions?

Eschew filters and "light" cigarettes; they just aren't cool.

Encourage your lover to smoke so you can both have ashtray breath.

Fearless
Smoker

WHO IS THIS BUTTON FOR?

Alcoholics.[1]

Heavy drinkers in denial.

PROVOCATIVE SUGGESTIONS

Celebrate the fact that your drug of choice—though as dangerous and addictive as any other—is cheap, socially acceptable, and almost universally available.

Cultivate friendships with teetotalers and ex-drinkers for the sole purpose of getting a ride home from parties and bars.

Drink to make other people interesting.[2]

1 Also for winos, boozers, barflies, alkies, piss artists, waste cases, plonkos, dredge-heads, shickers, soaks, rumpots, brewhounds, lushes, and aristocrats of the bottle of all nations, except countries such as Saudi Arabia where alcohol is prohibited—as it was in the USA, from 1920 to 1933.
2 A convincing reason to imbibe—attributed to George Jean Nathan.

WHO IS THIS BUTTON FOR?

Anyone chronically fixated on mobile devices.

Vacant-faced phonegazers.

PROVOCATIVE SUGGESTIONS

Look down now to avoid the anxiety of FOMO.[1]

Tap away in theaters and movies and ignore anyone calling you "Blueface."[2]

Your world may be small, but it is perfectly formed.

Swipe your screen to make this page disappear.

---

1   Fear Of Missing Out
2   A disrespectful term used to describe the eerie, blue lighting-up of your face by your phone in rooms darkened for movies, theater, concerts, operas, and stand-up comedy.

WHO IS THIS BUTTON FOR?

Cybernauts who spend an unhealthy amount of time online.[1]

Anyone who consciously or unconsciously prefers virtual reality to real life.

Screengazers who *know* that technology is absolute proof of human evolution.

PROVOCATIVE SUGGESTIONS

Like, tweet, and post your way to happiness.

Vaccinate yourself (and your square-faced lover) against your natural enemy, the virus.

Navigate safely back to planet Earth.

---

1   This addiction has several sub-types (e.g., cybersex addiction, online auction addiction, and addiction to online trading and gambling).

WHO IS THIS BUTTON FOR?

The intentionally late, the incompetently late, and the unconsciously late.

Rock stars and all other celebrities and latecomers.

PROVOCATIVE SUGGESTIONS

Take it easy and slow down! What's the rush?

Retain control by making others wait.

Atone for arriving late by leaving early.

KINDA:LATE

USUALLY:LATE

ALWAYS:LATE

DAMN:LATE

!@#$%:LATE

WHO IS THIS BUTTON FOR?

"Caffed-up" workaholics and students.[1]

Those who know which countries have the best coffee beans.

People on first-name terms with their baristas.

PROVOCATIVE SUGGESTIONS

Complete your daily tasks in the first 90 minutes of the day—while you're still buzzing.

Nag your friends to upgrade their percolators, espresso machines, and milk-frothers.

Look into the use of coffee enemas, yet another health benefit of coffee.[2]

---

1   Caffeine is probably second only to alcohol as the world's most popular drug.
2   Coffee is a source of antioxidants and has been mooted to reduce the risk of Parkinson's disease, cirrhosis of the liver, Alzheimer's disease, and dementia.

WHO IS THIS BUTTON FOR?

Loud bosses, spouses, and dictators.

Sergeants and other NCOs.

Rageaholics.

Parents.

PROVOCATIVE SUGGESTIONS

SCREAM, YELL AND SHOUT TO ENSURE YOU GET WHAT YOU WANT IN LIFE!

SHOUTING WORKS! THIS HAS BEEN PROVEN![1]

---

1   Every army in the world uses it in the basic training of recruits. QED.

WHO IS THIS BUTTON FOR?

People for whom real life can be a distraction from electronic intercourse.

Most other humans.

PROVOCATIVE SUGGESTIONS

Praise the heavens for an invention greater than the wheel![1]

Leverage your phone to avoid eye contact with real people.

When using hands-free, wearing the button is essential to convey to passersby that you are partaking in intelligent telecommunication, rather than psychotically talking to yourself.

Surely it's time to upgrade?

---

1   The cell phone is nonviolent while the wheel has blood on its tires.

WHO IS THIS BUTTON FOR?

Cokeheads, snow-birds, *shnarfers*[1], and other "wired" individuals.

PROVOCATIVE SUGGESTIONS

Be proud and grateful that you can afford to consume a substance more expensive than gold and seldom as pure.

When you're high, use your phone to record your conversations so that all the kind and wise things you say will be preserved.

Ask your doctor to prescribe the best sedatives to ease the pain of "coming down."[2]

Start saving for lawyers' fees, detox clinics and expensive bills from ear, nose and throat surgeons.[3]

---

[1] Onomatopeic South African slang for snorters of cocaine.

[2] In medically supervised dosage these can also give you a good night's sleep. Warning! Since addiction to tranquilizers is highly possible, remind your doctor to get you to sign a contract absolving him/her of all responsibility for this eventuality.

[3] Nasal reconstruction surgery isn't cheap and may not be covered by government or private medical insurance; check your policy!

WHO IS THIS BUTTON FOR?

Any needle artist injecting anything into their veins without official medical supervision.

Speedballers[1] and Snowballers.[2]

Junkies and other losers.

PROVOCATIVE SUGGESTIONS

Spend a little more for purity and clean needles.

Be proud of your ability to locate veins[3] that would turn any doctor green with...uh...envy.

Feel sanguine about outliving most of your friends.

1 Users who get high on a combination of heroin and cocaine.
2 Users whose first love is cocaine but need heroin to come down.
3 The art of putting a needle in a vein in order to extract blood is known as phlebotomy.

WHO IS THIS BUTTON FOR?

Gamblers of all shapes and sizes.

Day traders.

PROVOCATIVE SUGGESTIONS

Double up! It *almost* works as a system.

Place your trust in "gut feelings," astrological charts, psychic hotlines, tipsters, and the advice of financial pundits.

Don't feel guilty about that jewelry you had to sell during a bad spell; it never really suited your partner anyway.

WHO IS THIS BUTTON FOR?

Carriers of concealed weapons.

Cops and robbers.

Members of the National Rifle Association.

Armies.

PROVOCATIVE SUGGESTIONS

Stick to your guns but don't point them at your genitals.

Learn and repeatedly recite the Second Amendment in the Bill of Rights in the US Constitution.[1]

---

1   "A well-regulated Militia, being necessary to the security of a free State, the right of the people to keep and bear Arms, shall not be infringed."

WHO IS THIS BUTTON FOR?

Lazy people—maybe there's a better adjective to describe you guys but we can't be bothered to find it.[1]

Loafers and under-achievers.

PROVOCATIVE SUGGESTIONS

There is no food like fast food.[2]

Avoid work by wisely delegating all of it.

Always adopt the passive position while having sex.

---

1 However it is painless enough for us to quote *The New Penguin Thesaurus* (Penguin Books 2001 paperback edition p.347) LAZY adj slothful, idle, indolent, slack, workshy, inactive, inert, sluggish, torpid, lethargic, slow, languid, languorous. OPPOSITE industrious)

2 Only a click or call away from most of us nowadays.

WHO IS THIS BUTTON FOR?

Lounge lizards, lotus eaters, funkers and other "sitizens."

Do-littles favoring a sedentary lifestyle.

PROVOCATIVE SUGGESTIONS

Always buy the best quality slippers, loafers, tracksuits, sound system, television, cable channels, and broadband connection.

Never do anything if a machine can do it for you.

Tip those magnificent men on motorbikes who risk their lives to deliver your nutrition.

COUCH
POTATO

WHO IS THIS BUTTON FOR?

Loyal fans of the Western World's favorite hobby.[1]

Sentimental senior citizens who still watch mainstream television.

PROVOCATIVE SUGGESTIONS

Be grateful to the program sponsors whose expensive advertisements make television such awesome entertainment.

Feel privileged to be able to sit in an armchair and monitor our troubled world rather than take part in it.

---

1 You have to be loyal to eschew the internet in favor of what is dished up to you on television.

WHO IS THIS BUTTON FOR?

Armchair experts fixated on the latest trending topic or crisis.

People obsessed with watching history repeat itself.[1]

PROVOCATIVE SUGGESTIONS

Take advantage of our unprecedented access to news twenty-four seven.

Ensure that nobody ever accuses you of being ignorant of history.[2]

Conspiracy theories and fake news are worth investigating.

---

1   "We learn from history that we do not learn from history."—Georg Wilhelm Friedrich Hegel
2   Take heed of the words of George Santayana: "Those who cannot remember the past are condemned to repeat it"—and track history as it happens.

WHO IS THIS BUTTON FOR?

Fans spiritually and financially devoted to their heroes.

Viewers who curse, cheer, and boo at their TV screens and phones.

Worshippers at the great cathedrals of contemporary religion—sports stadiums.

PROVOCATIVE SUGGESTIONS

Relish the herd mentality by wearing your team's colors[1] every day.

Curb your sports budget by limiting your expenditure to 49% of your income.

Lose or win, your team is inherently superior to all other teams, so you're entitled to be an irritable pain in the butt when they are defeated by their inferiors.

Keep your sports widow sweet by buying her or him a trinket every now and then.

---

1 So what if the jerseys are garish, synthetic, and overpriced? It's your duty to give your team as much free advertising as possible.

WHO IS THIS BUTTON FOR?

Potheads and other stoners.

Patients prescribed tetrahydrocannabinol (THC) for medical reasons.

PROVOCATIVE SUGGESTIONS

Ensure that your refrigerator is well stocked with junk food at all times.

Use digital technology to improve your memory.

Move to a state or country where recreational cannabis[1] is pure, legal, available, and cheap.

Moderation never works.

1   The cannabis plant has long been perceived as a recreational drug. It is however acquiring an increasing number of recognized medicinal applications, and history shows it to be a plant with a great variety of industrial uses. *Popular Mechanics* reported in 1938: "Over 25,000 products can be manufactured from hemp, from cellophane to dynamite."

WHO IS THIS BUTTON FOR?

Those who would rather go without sex than chocolate.

Other chocoholics.

PROVOCATIVE SUGGESTIONS

Eat in secret to avoid sharing.

Take pride in your encyclopedic knowledge of the calorific world of chocolate.

Boast that research that has shown that chocolate:

a) is absolutely essential for the healthy sexual functioning of the human female.[1]

b) is good for your heart.[2]

---

1   Just kidding. This may be true, but it has not been proven.
2   "Oleic acid, a monounsaturated fat also found in olive oil, makes up one-third of the fat in chocolate and has been shown to be beneficial for heart health." (Journal of the American Dietetic Association, February 2003) As a doctor, I do feel a duty to remind you that obesity is a serious risk factor for diabetes, hypertension, arthritis, and certain cancers as well as coronary artery disease.

WHO IS THIS BUTTON FOR?

Users of the "love drug" and seekers of XTC.

Revelers, ravers, e-tards, and "molly" men, women, and anyone in between.

PROVOCATIVE SUGGESTIONS

Hello friendly, thirsty person with dilated pupils :-)

Start a campaign for purity.[1]

---

1 Pills sold as Ecstasy, Molly, E, XTC, X, Adam, beans, hug, clarity and lover's speed are seldom pure MDMA (3,4-methylenedioxy-N-methylamphetamine) and are usually cut with a variety of other drugs, which include ketamine, amphetamine, caffeine, ephedrine, flunitrazepam and others, as well as true poisons.

WHO IS THIS BUTTON FOR?

Grumblers, nitpickers, faultfinders, whiners, whingers, and other complainers.

PROVOCATIVE SUGGESTIONS

👎 and ⭐☆☆☆☆ at least an hour a day to help raise standards in our dystopian world.

Who says the only time to moan is when you are really enjoying sex?

CHAPTER 2: SEX, LOVE, AND RELATIONSHIPS

Doctors have a duty to restore health but medicine also requires us to relieve suffering. A vital factor affecting our health is the quality of our personal relationships. Single people often blame their unhappiness on not having secured the right partner. Many married couples have simply given up sex. Any doctor who takes the time to talk to his or her patients knows that sexual dissatisfaction is a frequent cause of unhappiness.

Some couples are fine until a four-letter word enters their lives—kids. Many may miss the good old days of being passionate lovers but are often distracted by another four-letter word—work. In-laws and money are the other two frequently mentioned anti-aphrodisiacs.

The harmony of family life has been roughed up by the demands of modern living. Family meals are out of fashion. There are many parents who "can't talk now" to their children. Before you know it, "now" becomes a few years ago, and your kids no longer want to talk to you!

Read on and you may be in danger of finding a comical button that provokes you to improve the quality of your relationships.

WHO IS THIS BUTTON FOR?

Anyone overusing poor parenting as an excuse for unhappiness.

Professionals who aid and abet the above.

Other transgressors of the Fifth Commandment.[1]

PROVOCATIVE SUGGESTIONS

Punish your parents for their errors by suing them, divorcing them, converting to a new religion, or buying yourself a big motorbike.

Continue to play the blame game but give your parents a break by letting siblings, children, friends, neighbors, teachers, therapists, politicians, the economy, and the weather share the blame for your suffering.

---

1 "Honor thy father and thy mother: that thy days may be long upon the land which the Lord thy God giveth thee." (Ex. 20:12, KJV)

WHO IS THIS BUTTON FOR?

Grown-up boys who see no reason to leave home.

"Men" in despair of ever finding a woman as wonderful as their mother.

Oedipus.

PROVOCATIVE SUGGESTIONS

Phone Mom now! Haven't you got some laundry to take round?[1]

Consider the possibility that your father may also have made a contribution.

1   In 2014 a UK survey of 2,739 adult men found that one in seven still had their mothers doing their laundry.

WHO IS THIS BUTTON FOR?

Lipstick girls in enticing gear.

Décolletage displayers.

Heavy petters who don't "go all the way."

PROVOCATIVE SUGGESTIONS

Revel in the sheer power of knowing what others want and not giving it to them.

Slap the face of anyone who has the nerve to paw you or make a suggestive remark when this button is in full view on your chest.

Be proud of teaching predatory men a valuable lesson in self-restraint in the face of temptation.

WHO IS THIS BUTTON FOR?

Prattlers, chatterers, jabberers, and other gossips.

PROVOCATIVE SUGGESTIONS

Take vengeance[1] on the hypocrites who love gossip but hate you for gossiping.

Master all social media platforms to reach the millions.

At least give your victims a chance to pay for your silence.

---

1   Verbal revenge behind their backs is your forte, of course.

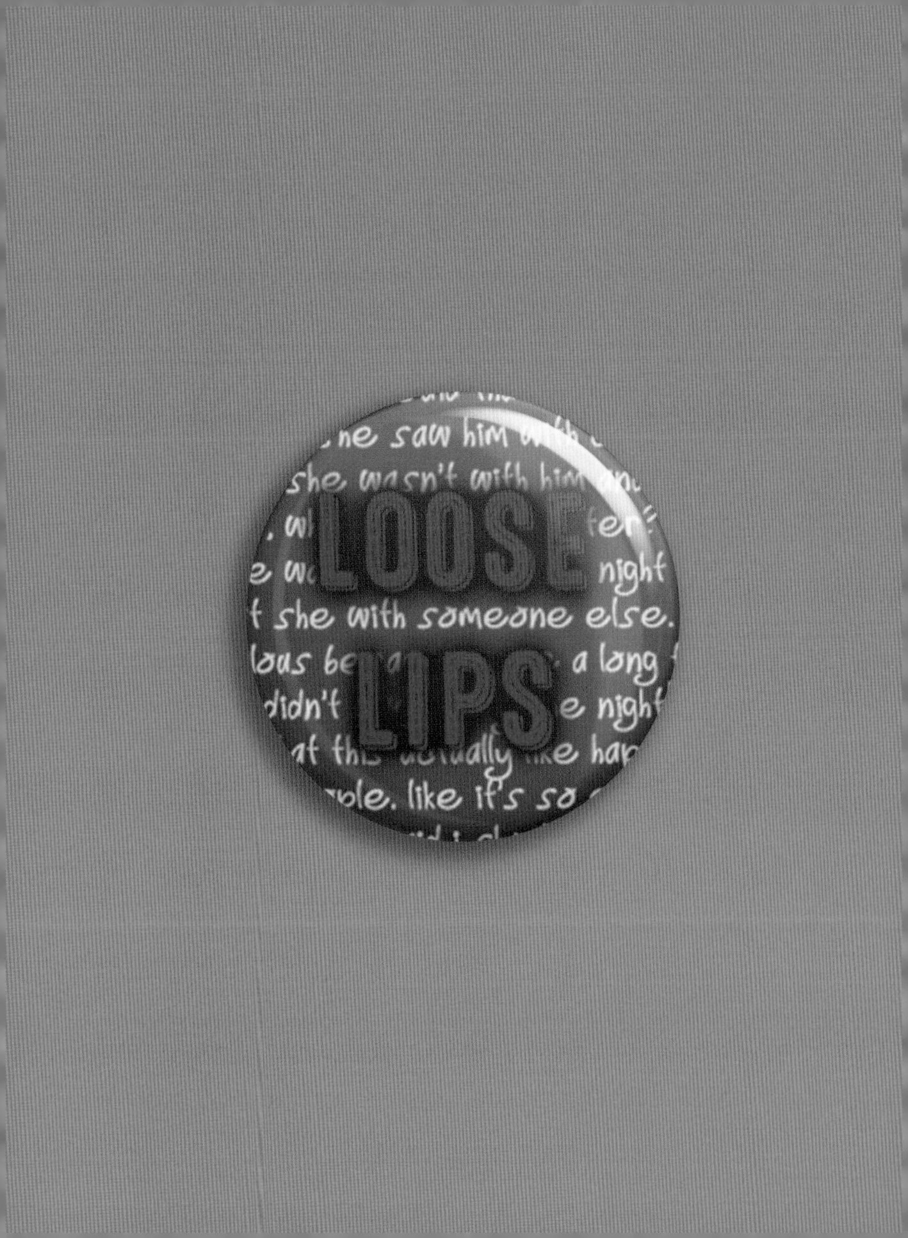
LOOSE
LIPS
she with someone else.

WHO IS THIS BUTTON FOR?

Winners in the genetic beauty stakes lottery.

Non-pretty people who are privileged in other ways.

PROVOCATIVE SUGGESTIONS

Wallow in it!

WHO IS THIS BUTTON FOR?

People who find that other people, for some reason, can never remember their names.

People who aren't recognized by others they have met, or been introduced to, or even slept with.

PROVOCATIVE SUGGESTIONS

Use Facebook to force people to refresh their memories of you.

Kooky clothes and absurd accessories may stimulate the power of recall in others.

WHO IS THIS BUTTON FOR?

Shy, lonely people with high sex drives.

PROVOCATIVE SUGGESTIONS

Whatever anybody says or thinks, you are practicing the safest sex known to humanity.

Don't worry; you're missing nothing except STDs, unwanted pregnancy, and icky sheets.

LIVES HERE

HORNY
RECLUSE

WHO IS THIS BUTTON FOR?

Connoisseurs of erotica.

Anyone who actually pays for internet porn.

PROVOCATIVE SUGGESTIONS

Admit that virtual sex is better than no sex at all.

Concede that virtual sex is often better than real sex.

Be proud of the fact that virtual sex is *safe sex*.

Feel no shame; you are a member of one of the most popular clubs on the planet.

Invite your partner to get in on the act.

WHO IS THIS BUTTON FOR?

Blue-balled guys too lazy or clueless to be nice enough to be rewarded with one.

Most people identifying as male.

PROVOCATIVE SUGGESTIONS

Become an expert at *giving* oral sex (or at least volunteer).

Guys: Kindness, thoughtfulness, praise, generosity, gentleness and timing of touch, frequent stroking, and massages are reliable routes to success—but the effort involved just won't be worth it.

Reminder for non-swallowers and dieters: It's only five to twenty-five calories per serving.

WHO IS THIS BUTTON FOR?

Most men—according to most women.

Anyone enslaved to their libido.

Tinderists.

F*ckaholics.

PROVOCATIVE SUGGESTIONS

Perfect your seduction skills because you need multiple partners to experience every position in the Kama Sutra.

You of all people must put rubber between yourself and life.

Sanctify your sex life by marrying a fellow sex addict.

WHO IS THIS BUTTON FOR?

Egotists, narcissists, and I-specialists.

Other self-centered people.

PROVOCATIVE SUGGESTIONS

Never drift too far from a mirror or selfie-stick.

Spend more time on social media keeping everyone up to date with your adventures.

No need to waste money on life insurance since it cannot benefit *you* in any way.

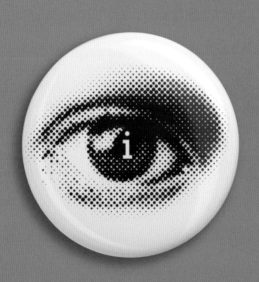

WHO IS THIS BUTTON FOR?

"FOG"[1] operators who misuse fear, emotion, guilt, and their "vulnerability" to manipulate and punish family, partners, and friends.

Anyone holding others to ransom, by threatening to rock the boat unless *their* immediate emotional needs are given top priority.

PROVOCATIVE SUGGESTIONS

Embark immediately on the following highly effective three-step program:

1. Arrest yourself.

2. Plead guilty.

3. Sentence yourself to life.

---

1   "FOG" (Fear Obligation Guilt) is an acronym coined by psychotherapist and author Susan Forward PhD, who also coined the term "emotional blackmail" to describe the features of the psychological dynamics occurring between the emotional blackmailer and the blackmailee.

WHO IS THIS BUTTON FOR?

Grovellers, shmoozers, ass-kissers, ass-lickers, bootlickers, assorted yes-men, and other sycophants.

Anyone unhealthily preoccupied with what others think of them.

PROVOCATIVE SUGGESTIONS

Continue to brown-nose your way to success.

Carry on serving the needs of people more deserving than you; we appreciate it.

To all requests: Just say yes!

WHO IS THIS BUTTON FOR?

Nondescript people who really have no right to exist.

Anyone in hiding, on the run, or in a witness protection programme.

Ghosts.

PROVOCATIVE SUGGESTIONS

Do your disappearing trick now.

Avoid crime; you are still visible to the police and CCTV.

Prove your existence and influence by voting in all elections.

WHO IS THIS BUTTON FOR?

Altruists and "altruists."

Chronic givers and "do-gooders" who *apparently* expect nothing in return for their wise advice and loving deeds.

PROVOCATIVE SUGGESTIONS

Ignore all allegations that you can be controlling, smothering, or suffocating.

Turn the other cheek to depreciators and ingrates.

WHO IS THIS BUTTON FOR?

Gold diggers.

Fortune hunters.

PROVOCATIVE SUGGESTIONS

Take comfort in knowing that many others have resorted to this time-honored strategy for becoming rich.

Feel smugly superior to the millions of people poorer than you—but just as unhappily married.

Keep in mind that things could be worse—you could have married for sex.[1]

---

1 Sex, unlike money, cannot be saved for a rainy day—such as the day you get divorced.

I
MARRIED
MONEY

WHO IS THIS BUTTON FOR?

Busy, industrious people who have no time for small talk.

People whose catchphrase is "Can I call you back?"

Parents frustrated with the stupid questions their kids seem to be asking all the time.

PROVOCATIVE SUGGESTIONS

Repeat over and over, "Time is money, time is money, time is money..."

Be patient: your children will leave home soon and stop bothering you with their childish comments.

WHO IS THIS BUTTON FOR?

The incarcerated, the trapped, the locked-down, and the caged.

Anyone imprisoned by the neurotic needs of others.

PROVOCATIVE SUGGESTIONS

Don't do anything rash; many caged animals die when suddenly released.

Conceal your predicament by discarding photographs that look like mugshots and never wearing orange clothes.

Improve your life by befriending your jailer.[1]

---

1 But always be aware of "capture bonding" a.k.a *The Stockholm Syndrome*

WHO IS THIS BUTTON FOR?

Anyone who thinks they've married the wrong person.

Married couples who lack a mutual interest in sex and pretty much everything else.

Adulterers.

PROVOCATIVE SUGGESTIONS

My heart goes out to you if you are unhappily married because I'm *happily* married and it's terrible!

Cement your marriage by having a few more kids.

Bear in mind that the first forty years of marriage are the hardest.

Be grateful that you are not being bled dry by a divorce lawyer—yet.

WHO IS THIS BUTTON FOR?

Married cheats, deceivers, liars, and philanderers.

PROVOCATIVE SUGGESTIONS

Enjoy! Naughty sex is the best!

Ignore your pesky conscience and just follow your animal instincts.

Digitally record all your adult(erous) sex sessions for further reference.[1]

Get the most out of your life before it is shredded by divorce lawyers.

---

1 These videos will be especially helpful if (a) your marriage falls apart and/or (b) your lover tries to blackmail you.

WHO IS THIS BUTTON FOR?

Those impoverished by divorce.

Those financially impoverished by divorce.

Those sexually impoverished by divorce.

PROVOCATIVE SUGGESTIONS

Perfect the art of the vituperative snipe.

Force your children to take sides in the ongoing argument with your ex.

Make your divorce an enriching experience.

If you don't get the financial settlement you always knew you deserved—sue your lawyers!

CHAPTER 3: HEALTH AND WELL-BEING

Our health—physical, mental, and spiritual—has a major influence on our happiness. Still, we don't always make rational decisions about our health or care for ourselves in the ways we should.

When suffering from life-threatening conditions such as meningitis or kidney failure, we tend to do what medical doctors advise us. However when facing less immediate challenges to our health, we're more selective about the advice we choose to follow. Is this because we simply don't like following orders?

How then can we help people who overeat, overwork, refuse or forget to take prescribed medication, and avoid exercise and relaxation? The buttons that follow exaggerate and satirize patterns of behavior that jeopardize our physical health. If you recognize yourself in any of these buttons, we hope you will see the funny side of the situation and prescribe a healthier lifestyle for yourself.

WHO IS THIS BUTTON FOR?

Shunners of medical doctors who prefer to consult Dr. Google and WebMD.

People determined to extract the absolute maximum value from their medical insurance.

Sufferers of Münchausen Syndrome.[1]

PROVOCATIVE SUGGESTIONS

Spend many hours online to keep up to date on the latest research on your various ailments.

Never take medical advice without getting a second and preferably third opinion. [2]

---

1 A rare psychiatric condition characterized by the search for medical care for feigned illnesses that tend to present with dramatic symptoms. This disorder is named after Baron Karl Friedrich Hieronymus von Münchausen (1720-1797). His fictionalized life adventures became popular books that were eventually made into movies. He did not, however, suffer personally from Münchausen Syndrome.

2 "Nobody should underestimate the contribution made to the medical profession by the Jewish people—in their capacity as *patients*."—Arnold Brown, comedian.

Professional
Patient

my symptoms|

WHO IS THIS BUTTON FOR?

Frequenters of health food stores.

Composers of long lists of vitamin, mineral, and other food supplements.

Owners of vitamin dispensers.

PROVOCATIVE SUGGESTIONS

Multivitamins, mineral complexes, and powdered foods are superior to fruit and vegetables because they are designed by top scientists.

Take care not to stain your underclothes with fluorescent yellow vitamin pee.

WHO IS THIS BUTTON FOR?

Iron-pumping, protein-packing fitness freaks.

Locker room show-boaters.

PROVOCATIVE SUGGESTIONS

Wallow in the admiration of your lycra-clad fans of all sexes.

Medical opinion is on your side so ensure you get a discount on your health insurance.

Stay strong, swift, and sexy forever!

WHO IS THIS BUTTON FOR?

Fit girls and sportswomen.

Female flexors, stretchers, and spinners.

PROVOCATIVE SUGGESTIONS

Beach? Who needs sand getting everywhere when you can show off your gorgeous body to gawking hunks in a gym?

WHO IS THIS BUTTON FOR?

The BIG APPETITED.

Ravenous people whose refrigerators rear back in horror when they see them coming.

Thin folk filling up on fake food a lot.

Yes, this button can have a sexual connotation.

PROVOCATIVE SUGGESTIONS

Eat now!

Never miss a free lunch.

WHO IS THIS BUTTON FOR?

The overweight[1] and obese.[2]

Anorexics and bulimics.

PROVOCATIVE SUGGESTIONS

Try to become *more* infatuated with food.

Pre-empt vile fat-shamers by cheerfully wearing the button.

You're perfect the way you are. Just join NAAFA.[3]

Immigrate to a country where the rotund enjoy high social status.

---

1   A BMI greater than or equal to 25 (World Health Organization [WHO] definition)
2   A BMI greater than or equal to 30 (WHO definition)
3   NAAFA: National Association to Advance Fat Acceptance.

WHO IS THIS BUTTON FOR?

Weight watchers and slimmers of all shapes and sizes.

PROVOCATIVE SUGGESTIONS

Trust that every new diet will be a scientific breakthrough.

Diet—binge—new diet—same binge—another new diet—same binge…

Try the Food Porn Diet: Instead of eating, tune into Food Network shows and indulge yourself.

WHO IS THIS BUTTON FOR?

Thin, slim, skinny ones.

Models and other girls and boys in danger of being mistaken as sufferers of eating disorders.

PROVOCATIVE SUGGESTIONS

Never trust a mirror; you're definitely fatter than your reflection!

Take pity on your envious, overweight girlfriends.[1]

Anyone saying they prefer voluptuous, curvaceous girls is not to be believed.

---

1 That probably means *all* your female friends.

WHO IS THIS BUTTON FOR?

All females with these social assets.

PROVOCATIVE SUGGESTIONS

If you've got it flaunt it!

Where nature does not deliver, plastic surgeons say: "Yes we can!"

Take pity on those who go into trance as they stare or try too hard *not* to look at them.

For the formerly well-endowed: Hope you have fond memories of the good old days.

WHO IS THIS BUTTON FOR?

Follicularly challenged males.

Men walking and talking under a wig or toupee.

Men whose comb-overs make their heads look like barcodes.

PROVOCATIVE SUGGESTIONS

Hairpiece technology is now so advanced that nobody will ever suspect the hair you purchased isn't really yours.

Follicular unit transplantation is expensive but one of the great medical advances of recent times.

Revel in the knowledge that many women still believe the myth that bald men have higher levels of testosterone.[1]

---

1   Male-pattern baldness is due to high levels of DHT (dihydrotestosterone), which actually *doesn't* affect libido or sexual prowess, but shhhh...

WHO IS THIS BUTTON FOR?

Big boys and mentulated men.

Porn stars.[1]

Donkeys.

PROVOCATIVE SUGGESTIONS

Give thanks for an attribute coveted by most men and a few women too.

Be proud that you will always be King—of the locker room.

Take pity on the remaining 95% of the male population who are less biologically gifted than you.

---

1 Who may daunt viewers or leave them with unrealistic expectations.

WHO IS THIS BUTTON FOR?

Smokers.

The obese.

Exercise avoiders.

Lovers of animal fats.

Noncompliant diabetics and hypertensives.

The seriously stressed out.[1]

PROVOCATIVE SUGGESTIONS

Postpone all lifestyle changes until your heart starts giving you danger signals.[2]

1　There is plenty of evidence to suggest that stress is bad for your heart and even some suggesting that laughter is good for it.

2　For example: Heart attack, stroke, or angina. You may also at least *consider* adopting healthier habits after abnormal test results (e.g., EKG, cardiac stress test, coronary artery CT scan, a dangerously high cholesterol level, and persistently high blood pressure).

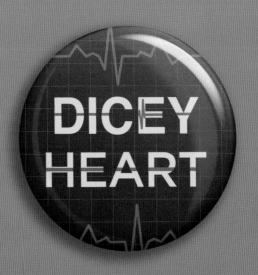

WHO IS THIS BUTTON FOR?

Wearers of false smiles and other masks.

Loyal patients of plastic surgeons.

PROVOCATIVE SUGGESTIONS

Fake it, fake it until you make it!

Study not only facial expressions but also the speech, behavior, and lives of the greatest conmen and flimflam men and women of all time.

Take pride in having the courage (and the money) to correct Nature's mistakes.[1]

---

1   Choices include liposuction, facial peels, facial filling, buttock tucks, face lifts, botox injections, breast augmentation, breast reduction, penile enlargement surgery etc; contact your local plastic surgeon for more information.

WHO IS THIS BUTTON FOR?

People carrying more than their fair share of emotional pain.

Silent sufferers who carry on bravely as if all was normal.

PROVOCATIVE SUGGESTIONS

Never speak of your pain because a problem shared is a problem doubled.

Nothing wrong with the occasional temper tantrum.

Be creative! Many great musicians, artists, and writers are fueled by angst.

WHO IS THIS BUTTON FOR?

The hospitalized.

Graduates and dropouts from rehab clinics and twelve-step programs.

PROVOCATIVE SUGGESTIONS

The best time to start getting better is—tomorrow.

"Falling off the wagon" and "the revolving door" are useful clichés to hang on to.

Avoid others in recovery; they are a bad influence.

.

WHO IS THIS BUTTON FOR?

Perfectionists.

Fastidious people.

The overtidy.

PROVOCATIVE SUGGESTIONS

Use a spirit balance to ensure that the pictures on your walls are all level.

A brief study of chaos theory may put things into perspective—if not order—for you.

Being impeccable is exhausting, so make sure you get enough sleep.

WHO IS THIS BUTTON FOR?

Soft speakers, low-talkers, mumblers, and whisperers.

The insecure.

Snorers.

PROVOCATIVE SUGGESTIONS

Low talkers: Are you a man or a mouse? Squeak up![1]

The insecure: The world has plenty of loudmouths but is desperately short of intelligent listeners like yourself.

Snorers: Assert your inalienable right to a fair share of oxygen, even when you are asleep.

---

[1]   At least have mercy on the hard of hearing.

WHO IS THIS BUTTON FOR?

Daydreamers, meditators, and stargazers.

The hypnotized and the mesmerized.

People in love.

Psychedelic revelers.

Anyone spellbound by beauty.

PROVOCATIVE SUGGESTIONS

Enjoy the haze.

The world? What world?

Whatever you do, don't snap out of it!

WHO IS THIS BUTTON FOR?

Survivors of near-death experiences.

Rebirthing[1] enthusiasts.

The reincarnated.

PROVOCATIVE SUGGESTIONS

Wishing you a better life going forward.

Wishing you a better life next time around.

---

1   Rebirthing is a holistic therapy using a breathing technique.

WHO IS THIS BUTTON FOR?

Anyone less than physically healthy, sexually satisfied, emotionally sound, and financially secure.

US citizens actively exercising their inalienable right to pursue happiness.[1]

PROVOCATIVE SUGGESTIONS

Never let your personal life get in the way of your career.

Maintain your addictions at all costs.

More is always possible.[2]

---

1 "We hold these truths to be self-evident, that all men are created equal, that they are endowed by their Creator with certain unalienable Rights, that among these are Life, Liberty and the pursuit of Happiness." (*The Declaration of Independence*, July 4, 1776)

2 After decades pondering the important question "What do women want?" Frank Farrelly, the founder of Provocative Therapy, finally figured out the answer: "More!"

CHAPTER 4: WORK, POWER, AND MONEY

If you love your work, then it shouldn't feel like work at all. For those who have found their true vocation in life, it may be difficult to know whether they are good at what they do because they love their work or whether they love their work because they are so good at it.

Many people though, while grateful to have a source of income, do not enjoy their jobs at all but feel compelled to keep at them out of sheer necessity, commitment, or habit. There are two types of unhappy workers: those who genuinely have no choice and those who *think* they have no choice. It's not easy to help the former, but if you're the latter, you're an ideal candidate to reflect on what might be holding you back.

The stress of modern work life can often activate the worst parts of us in relation to power, money, and status. These buttons aim to lampoon and interrupt some disconcerting behavioral patterns that frequently emerge in the workplace.

Do you see part of yourself in any of them? If so, our advice is to ignore any feelings this provokes and get back to work!

WHO IS THIS BUTTON FOR?

Anyone unnecessarily spending many valuable hours getting to and from work.

PROVOCATIVE SUGGESTIONS

Cheer up and sing along with the Seven Dwarfs:

"Heigh-ho, heigh-ho, it's off to work we go.

We work all day, we get no pay,

Heigh-ho, heigh-ho, heigh-ho."

WHO IS THIS BUTTON FOR?

Wage slaves and disgruntled jobholders.

Workers required to urinate into a bottle.

Honey bees.

PROVOCATIVE SUGGESTIONS

Always *appear* to be busy.

Grovel before your superiors and kick the backsides of your subordinates.

Give thanks daily for not being unemployed.

WHO IS THIS BUTTON FOR?

The new princes and princesses of the universe.

Super-brained masters and mistresses of coding, screens, and keyboards.

Anyone who can design an app.

PROVOCATIVE SUGGESTIONS

Convert your exceptionally high IQ and narrow broadband of interest into big money.

Avoid the evil of digital terrorism of any kind.

Cash in now! The ever-younger lions of coding are hot on your trail!

WHO IS THIS BUTTON FOR?

People digitally-available twenty-four seven.[1]

Anyone plugged into a repetitive, predictable, daily life.[2]

Automatons and others under remote control.

PROVOCATIVE SUGGESTIONS

Obey![3]

You are hereby absolved from making any personal, ethical decisions. Do your duty as any good android should.

Be happy, the new world order desperately needs "people" like you.

---

1   Never, ever, ever switch off your cell phone.
2   There's a lot to be said for such a life. Ask any ant.
3   *The Three Laws of Robotics* (formulated in 1940 by Isaac Asimov and John W. Campbell):
    First law: A robot may not injure a human being, or, through inaction, allow a human being to come to harm.
    Second law: A robot must obey orders given it by human beings, except where such orders would conflict with the first law.
    Third law: A robot must protect its own existence as long as such protection does not conflict with the first or second laws.

WHO IS THIS BUTTON FOR?

Those who unhealthily sacrifice their own needs in order to serve others.

People who look their best when carrying a tray.

PROVOCATIVE SUGGESTIONS

Enjoy being a servant.[1]

Keep in mind that you are almost as entitled to being served as anyone else.

There is no yoga quite like Karma yoga.[2]

---

1 I serve; therefore I am.
2 "Karma yoga is a system of ethics and religion intended to attain freedom through unselfishness and good works. The Karma yogi need not believe in any doctrine whatsoever. He may not believe even in God, may not ask what his soul is, nor think of any metaphysical speculation. He has his own special aim of realizing selflessness, and he has to work it out himself. Every moment of his life must be realization, because he has to solve by mere work, without the help of doctrine or theory, the very same problem to which the Jnâni applies his reason and inspiration and the Bhakta his love."—Swami Vivekananda

WHO IS THIS BUTTON FOR?

Humble folk unashamed to be downtrodden.

Those who complain endlessly about how colleagues, family, and friends treat them badly, take advantage of them, and don't give them enough respect etc. etc.

Homer Simpson.

PROVOCATIVE SUGGESTIONS

Learn how to shuffle backward out of a room, rubbing your hands obsequiously as you bow to your superiors.

Out yourself as a masochist and admit your perverse delight in the way you are being oppressed.

Think what a mess the world would be if everyone were bossy and assertive.

WHO IS THIS BUTTON FOR?

Slaves, serfs, androids, and robots.

The Economy, Crime, Drugs (legal and illegal), Pensions, Violence, Epidemics, Health Insurance, and Global Warming…not.

Tamed animals.

PROVOCATIVE SUGGESTIONS

Follow the leader—whoever he, she, it or they may be.

Be proud of sharing the herd mentality.

Bleat the populist "wisdom" of your time and place.

Avoid research, debate, and independent thought, all of which can lead you astray.

WHO IS THIS BUTTON FOR?

Informers of all kinds—working for good or evil.

Anyone in the surveillance or "intelligence" industries.

Voyeurs, snitches, and dobbers.

Moles and rats.

PROVOCATIVE SUGGESTIONS

Luxuriate in the moral superiority that entitles you to lie to most of the people most of the time for the greater good.

Retire and join a high-stakes poker school where you can legitimize the deceitful games you love to play.

WHO IS THIS BUTTON FOR?

Doctors.

Corrupt politicians, shyster lawyers, bent builders, shady insurance salespeople, and telemarketers with "only two ____ left."

Con artists.

The Mafia.

The Devil.

PROVOCATIVE SUGGESTIONS

Trust doctors, trust God[1]—and distrust everyone else.

Practice hard at looking innocent and hiding your duplicitous body language.[2]

---

1   The US Treasury has wisely seen fit to dispense this advice on all American currency.
2   Such as twitches, tics, trembling hands, dilated pupils, clearing of the throat, and other examples of what poker players call "tells."

WHO IS THIS BUTTON FOR?

Business executives who "steal" without quite breaking the letter of the law.

Clued-in employees and associates of the above, such as their lawyers and accountants.

Tax "avoiders."

Those a little too easily convinced that they have "good reason" for taking possession of other people's property.

Banks.

PROVOCATIVE SUGGESTIONS

Sleep well; your conscience is clear.[1]

Expunge lingering guilt; it's not your fault that the mugs you ripped off are now bankrupt.

---

1   The small print was explicit and they should have read it. It is well known that a fool and his money are soon parted. If you hadn't taken it, someone else would have.

WHO IS THIS BUTTON FOR?

Stone-faced men and women of big business.

Anyone feeling the burden of being held responsible for profit and loss.

Venture capitalists and those with high stock market exposure.

PROVOCATIVE SUGGESTIONS

Never smile; serious money is no laughing matter.

It's a badge of honor to look ten years older than you are.[1]

Don't forget your annual visit to the cardiologist.

Why are you wasting your time reading this nonsense instead of working?

---

1 Looking mature is good for business.

WHO IS THIS BUTTON FOR?

Finger pointers.

The censorious.

PROVOCATIVE SUGGESTIONS

Keep at it! Yours is the toughest of jobs, but somebody's got to do something about the moronic inferno[1] out there.

Ignore anyone who appreciates your motives but wishes you'd go and practice on somebody else.

---

1   Pejorative term for modern society coined by Wyndham Lewis.

I CRITIC IZE

WHO IS THIS BUTTON FOR?

The vengeful, the greedy, and other "victims."

Anyone collaborating with a lawyer in the search for easy money.

Certain types of lawyers (you know who you are).

PROVOCATIVE SUGGESTIONS

If in doubt, litigate.

Enjoy your symbiotic relationship with the legal profession; lawyers need you as much as you need them.

Follow the example of many successful criminals and become an amateur lawyer yourself.[1]

---

1   "Make crime pay. Become a lawyer."—Will Rogers

WHO IS THIS BUTTON FOR?

People and pets comprehensively covered by premium insurance policies.[1]

Victims of "What if? merchants" (a.k.a. insurance salespeople).

Fraudsters who don't see exaggerated claims as criminal offences.[2]

PROVOCATIVE SUGGESTIONS

Never make an actual claim; insurance companies don't like it and will punish you severely by skyrocketing your premiums.

Increase your life insurance to the max; your loved ones may miss you, but there is solace in hard cash.

In our risk-averse society, it is certainly better to be safe than sorry.[3]

---

1 Including fire, theft, household accidents, personal injury, car, unemployment, malpractice (especially for doctors), travel, war, terrorism, plagues and pandemics, alien abduction, and of course medical insurance for you, your family, and all your pets. This list is far from comprehensive, but your broker(s) will fill in the gaps. Ask them also to insure you against as many "acts of God" as possible.

2 After all, insurance companies employ actuaries, who include people like you when assessing risk and calculating premiums for you and (unfortunately) the rest of us.

3 All encapsulated truths (a.k.a. clichés) are obviously valuable life lessons.

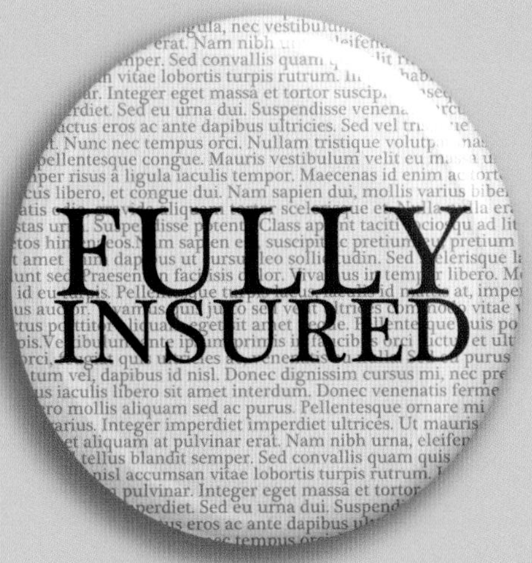
FULLY
INSURED

WHO IS THIS BUTTON FOR?

Consumers of cool products.

PROVOCATIVE SUGGESTIONS

If the best homes, cars, and holidays are out of reach, at least buy the best devices and gadgets.

Be proud of not settling for anything but the best.

WHO IS THIS BUTTON FOR?

Shopaholics and sufferers of Compulsive Buying Disorder.

People in retail therapy.

PROVOCATIVE SUGGESTIONS

BUY NOW! The Economy desperately needs people like you!

Never commit the sin of missing a bargain.

WHO IS THIS BUTTON FOR?

People whose partners and dependents assume they are money-making machines.

Parents whose children only visit them when they need money.

PROVOCATIVE SUGGESTIONS

Never forget your responsibility to the people who depend on your handouts.

You will be judged by the quality of your family's clothes, cars, and vacations; spend accordingly.

Inform all the freeloaders and leeches that you have a cash-flow crisis and are in desperate need of a loan yourself.[1]

---

1 Always remember that even ATMs occasionally run out of money or go wrong and refuse to cough up. Why should you be expected to perform any better?

WHO IS THIS BUTTON FOR?

Anyone who owes anybody anything.

High-living folk who never let the limitations of their income interfere with their lifestyle.

The US economy (and that of most other countries).

PROVOCATIVE SUGGESTIONS

Consolidate your debts on to a single credit card.[1]

Be cheerful—it's not you but your bank that has a problem!

---

1   It may cost a little more, but *one* angry creditor is a lot easier to deal with (administratively and legally speaking).

WHO IS THIS BUTTON FOR?

People who feel sorry for themselves.

The financially challenged.

Sufferers of "poverty consciousness."

PROVOCATIVE SUGGESTIONS

Mingle with people less fortunate than yourself.

Disguise your poverty by keeping your hair and shoes clean at all times.

Granted, the love of money is the root of all evil—but...

WHO IS THIS BUTTON FOR?

Idealists on the verge of making some necessary compromises.

Artists and musicians about to get into bed with advertising agencies.

Anyone finally realizing that in business, honesty may not always be the best policy.

PROVOCATIVE SUGGESTIONS

Integrity, morality, authenticity, and decency are fine—but they don't pay the bills, do they?

You should have done what you are doing now a long, long time ago.

Lament the fact that you have but one soul to sell.

WHO IS THIS BUTTON FOR?

Souls who sensed it was wrong to put their signatures on the dotted line but signed anyway.

Politicians enriched by politics.

Talented artists who went commercial.

People who gave up on "following their bliss."[1]

PROVOCATIVE SUGGESTIONS

Oh, no! It's too late to do anything except make another pact with the Devil.

The good news is that you'll find it a lot easier to sell out on everything else now.

If you ever need consolation or cheering up, phone your accountant.

---

1   "My general formula for my students is 'Follow your bliss. Find where it is, and don't be afraid to follow it.'"—Joseph Campbell, *The Power of Myth*. If we do not sell out on following this path, we could have a meaningful life. As Campbell says: "One way or another, we all have to find what best fosters the flowering of our humanity in this contemporary life, and dedicate ourselves to that." And if we don't, we can still aspire to being almost happy.

WHO IS THIS BUTTON FOR?

Misers, scrooges, and tightfisted cheapskates.

Alimony cheats.

PROVOCATIVE SUGGESTIONS

Don't buy this button! Print it, cut it out, and wear it—for nothing.

Saving is financially superior to giving.

Squirrels are the kings of the jungle.

WHO IS THIS BUTTON FOR?

Children of rich parents inconsiderately staying alive and irrationally refusing to hand over the money now.

Dependent descendants who let life slip by while they wait and wait and wait…

PROVOCATIVE SUGGESTIONS

Abandon all thoughts of getting rid of your parents.

Be meticulously and competitively attentive to your parents' every need.[1]

Borrow luxuriously against the collateral of your future inheritance.

---

1   It's not unheard of for parents to leave their money to animals instead of their own children.

WAITING
TO
INHERIT

CHAPTER 5: BUTTONS FOR ASSORTED PURPOSES

Okay, it's just possible that you've reached this far without being labeled by a button. You've recognized buttons that suit friends and family but have yet to spot a button that mirrors an aspect of yourself that isn't serving you well.

So maybe your life is pretty good. Perhaps you are successful, rich, carefree, satisfied, elegant, charming, fulfilled, witty, sexy, and even famous? But the question remains: Are you happy? Maybe you are almost happy?

Then again, for you there may be more important things in life to pursue than mere happiness. Do the words moral, religious, or spiritual apply to you? How about authentic, enlightened, or self-realized? Perhaps you have even transcended happiness?

Instead of focusing on specific issues that cause unhappiness, the buttons that follow reflect archetypal states of being that are less than happy. Many of these satirical buttons reflect views that we have of ourselves or that others may have of us.

Just a few more pages of buttons to flip through—but having escaped provocation for so long, perhaps now is the time to stop reading this book?

WHO IS THIS BUTTON FOR?

The mindful, the meditative, and other seekers.

Anyone in pursuit of self-realization.

Evolved people still waiting for a spiritual breakthrough.

PROVOCATIVE SUGGESTIONS

Go ego go!

Exercise empathy and compassion for materialists, hedonists, and narcissists because there but for the grace of God go you.

WHO IS THIS BUTTON FOR?

Sports heroes, politicians, pop idols, TV and movie stars, and other VIPs with an "attitude problem."

All children.

Demanders of preferential treatment.

PROVOCATIVE SUGGESTIONS

Avoid regular people who cannot appreciate the "special needs" of an icon such as you.

Condescendingly belittle, fire, or sue anyone disputing your entitlement to privilege.

Always travel first class. If you can't afford it, this button doesn't really suit you.

WHO IS THIS BUTTON FOR?

Kings, Queens, aristocrats, and other bluebloods.

Stars of movies, sports, and music.

Celebrities, grandees, and leading lights.

The haughty, arrogant, and overconfident.

Snobs.

Doctors.[1]

PROVOCATIVE SUGGESTIONS

Give yourself a break; everyone knows it's tough at the top.

Smile smugly as the common folk enjoy their bread and circuses.[2]

Explore your inferiority complex.[3]

---

1   Q: What's the difference between God and a doctor?
    A: God doesn't think he's a doctor.

2   Or as the Roman poet Juvenal put it, "a simplistic motivation of common people."

3   The term "inferiority complex" is based on the work of the psychoanalyst Alfred Adler (1870–1937). A contemporary of Freud, Adler believed that when low self-esteem is ignored, it can lead to various compensatory behaviors and personality disorders. His most well-known work is *Understanding Human Nature* (Garden City Publishers, 1927).

WHO IS THIS BUTTON FOR?

People who have made up their minds and prefer not to be confused by facts.

Perfectionists who see things in black and white and abhor all fifty shades of gray.

Other self-righteous people.

Parents.

PROVOCATIVE SUGGESTIONS

Men: Ask yourself repeatedly: "Do I want to be right or do I want to get laid?"

Women: Enhance your social status by reminding everyone that "I told you so."

Parents: Vigorously exploit your absolute authority—while you've still got it.

WHO IS THIS BUTTON FOR?

Those unpersuaded by reason or love.

Oxen.

PROVOCATIVE SUGGESTIONS

Clench your jaw and tense your muscles as you hold on to your position.

Never ever be acquiescent, agreeable, amenable, compliant, flexible, pliable, relenting, or yielding.

Dig your heels in further! You're in for the long haul here.

WHO IS THIS BUTTON FOR?

Anyone, anywhere, prejudiced in any way against any skin color.[1]

Those who expect less of other races and ethnicities.

Xenophobes.

PROVOCATIVE SUGGESTIONS

Vigorously campaign for National Brotherhood Week to be brought back.

Never be embarrassed to say: "Some of my best friends are..."

---

1 Particularly covertly and including prejudice against one's own race.

WHO IS THIS BUTTON FOR?

Anyone still unprovoked by a button.

Repudiators of reality.

Ostriches.

PROVOCATIVE SUGGESTIONS

Turn this page immediately!

Unlike medicine, psychotherapy, law, and accountancy, denial is always free.

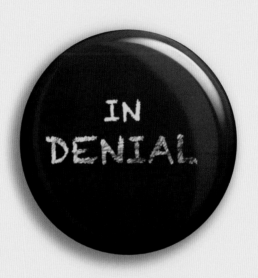

WHO IS THIS BUTTON FOR?

Intellectually and morally superior people who are fully conscious of how bad "they" (i.e. most of the rest of us) really are.

Virtue-signalers.

PROVOCATIVE SUGGESTIONS

Stick it to the man!

"They" (the unwoke) are the problem but you are the solution!

Nessun dorma!

WHO IS THIS BUTTON FOR?

Negators, dismissers, rollers of eyebrows, and other esteem-busters.

Masters of passive aggression.

Those whose company usually lowers the mood.

PROVOCATIVE SUGGESTIONS

Continue to overturn, refute, annul, undo, quash, overthrow, nullify, abrogate, undermine, and discredit humanity for its own benefit.

Always remember that people can benefit enormously from listening to your put-downs.

WHO IS THIS BUTTON FOR?

Those for whom the glass is almost always half empty.

Negativity addicts and other pessimists.

Eeyore.

PROVOCATIVE SUGGESTIONS

To avoid disappointment in life, keep your expectations really low.

Constantly repeat your mantra: "No, I can't!"

WHO IS THIS BUTTON FOR?

People who believe they would be happy if only certain conditions were met.

People convinced they would be happy if they could just rewrite the past.

Dreamers, enviers, and coveters.[1]

PROVOCATIVE SUGGESTIONS

Don't forget to buy a Lotto ticket! [2]

Cosmic Ordering is worth a try.

---

1 "Thou shalt not covet thy neighbor's house, thou shalt not covet thy neighbor's wife, nor his manservant, nor his maidservant, nor his ox, nor his ass, nor any thing that is thy neighbor's." (Exod. 20:17, KJV)
2 By far the best way to ensure you avoid catastrophic disappointment is to buy them online in advance. It is an undisputed fact that the more tickets you buy, the greater the chance of your dreams coming true.

WHO IS THIS BUTTON FOR?

Those fortunate enough to be under Divine Guidance.

Opponents of secular fundamentalism.

Proselytizers.

PROVOCATIVE SUGGESTIONS

Upgrade your megaphone.

Never forget that all you are saying is: "Give prayer a chance."

Sleep less to liberate more time to convert heathens.

WHO IS THIS BUTTON FOR?

Guilty absconders from a religious upbringing.

Transgressors of holy texts.

Fornicators and infidels.

PROVOCATIVE SUGGESTIONS

Repent now![1]

Consider converting to a religion that is more compatible with your lifestyle.

Conscience is nonsense.[2]

---

1   Confession, prayer, fasting, and flagellation are all sacred methods of atonement.
2   "The goal of psychotherapy is to make the unconscious conscience of the patient conscious."—Dr. E. K. Ledermann

WHO IS THIS BUTTON FOR?

Patriots: Domestic and global.

Sports fans at international events.[1]

PROVOCATIVE SUGGESTIONS

Hold your head high, as befits a member of the Almighty's "almost chosen people." [2]

Be polite and applaud the nations who excelled in coming second and third.

God bless America!

---

1 Especially the Ryder Cup, where you can hear full-throated golf fans roar the words on this button.

2 "I am exceedingly anxious that this Union, the Constitution, and the liberties of the people shall be perpetuated in accordance with the original idea for which that struggle was made, and I shall be most happy indeed if I shall be an humble instrument in the hands of the Almighty, and of this, his almost chosen people, for perpetuating the object of that great struggle."—Abraham Lincoln, February 21, 1861; speech to the New Jersey Senate

WHO IS THIS BUTTON FOR?

Countries in dispute.[1]

Couples in dispute.

Anybody else in dispute.

PROVOCATIVE SUGGESTIONS

Leaders of countries: You know you are right and therefore thousands of your subjects will happily lay down their lives for you.

Couples in dispute: If you haven't yet employed expensive lawyers, you haven't even begun to fight!

Others in arguments: The theory and practice of war are applicable in every adversarial situation.[2]

Let all humans unite and wage war on our common enemy—the mosquito.[3]

1 This button fires a satirical harpoon at the bellicose subself that advocates violence as a solution to anything. When all else has failed, it might be time to try reverse psychology.
2 *The Art of War* by Sun Tzu (approx. 500 BCE) is a classic text.
3 These vile insects, by spreading diseases such as yellow fever, dengue, Zika, and particularly malaria, kill over a million of us a year. War Now on humanity's most deadly foe!

WHO IS THIS BUTTON FOR?

People who let fear thwart them from leading a full life.

Risk minimizers.

The overinsured.

PROVOCATIVE SUGGESTIONS

It's rational to be overcautious! Just read the papers, watch TV, or go online to prove to yourself just how dangerous the world really is.

Isn't it time to give your insurance broker a call?

Building a nuclear fallout shelter is not as stupid as it sounds.[1]

---

1 Consider the mentality, wisdom, and compassion of those who have their fingers on the button these days.

WHO IS THIS BUTTON FOR?

Skeptics, iconoclasts, and postmodernists.[1]

Logical, reasonable people who eschew intuition, gut feelings, and all things mystical.

The militantly scientific and scientismic.[2]

Those who prefer ideas to people.

PROVOCATIVE SUGGESTIONS

Base your choice of a wife, husband, or partner on objective evidence rather than on subjective feelings (e.g., love).

Avoid religious texts, but do study philosophy, deeply.[3]

---

1   "Postmodernism is a late-twentieth-century movement in the arts, architecture, and criticism that was a departure from modernism. Postmodernism includes skeptical interpretations of culture, literature, art, philosophy, history, economics, architecture, fiction, and literary criticism. It is often associated with deconstruction and post-structuralism because its usage as a term gained significant popularity at the same time as twentieth-century post-structural thought." (Wikipedia)

2   Scientism: Pejorative term for the belief that the methods of natural science, or the categories and things recognized in natural science, form the only proper elements in any philosophical or other inquiry (Oxford Dictionary of Philosophy, Oxford University Press. pp. 331–32).

3   *The Critique of Pure Reason*, by Immanuel Kant, is a good place to start and should ideally be read in the original German.

WHO IS THIS BUTTON FOR?

Moderns and postmoderns who know that nothing means anything.

PROVOCATIVE SUGGESTIONS

None.

WHO IS THIS BUTTON FOR?

People who only speak other people's lines.

Thespians, actors, and performers who find it impossible to leave the stage.

Sports stars attempting to dupe referees and umpires.

Politicians.[1]

PROVOCATIVE SUGGESTIONS

In order to fool all the people all the time, take professional acting lessons.

Never let people get to know the real you—they may not like it.

---

1 Q: How can you tell if a politician is lying?
  A: His lips are moving. (Old joke)

WHO IS THIS BUTTON FOR?

People who believe that Science Rules!

Disillusioned artists and artisans.

Anyone free of the burden of aesthetics.

PROVOCATIVE SUGGESTIONS

Avoid all pretentious cultural events (e.g. art exhibitions, poetry readings, music recitals, book signings, arthouse movies, guided tours of ancient ruins, ballet, and especially, opera).

Destroy all those useless artifacts in your house.

Just because you don't like art doesn't mean it can't be a good investment (to be kept out of sight and in a bank vault, of course).

Do not look at sunsets or starlit skies.

WHO IS THIS BUTTON FOR?

Like, people who like overuse and misuse the word "like" kind-of-like a bit too often for anyone who, like, values the English language.

Dictionaries.[1]

PROVOCATIVE SUGGESTIONS

Like what's wrong with, like, parroting the word "like" to like describe things?

You are like normal—like, you know what I mean?

---

1   The word "like" is so frequently used colloquially to describe objects and actions that it deserves to be included in all dictionaries as a non-qualifying adjective and non-modifying adverb.

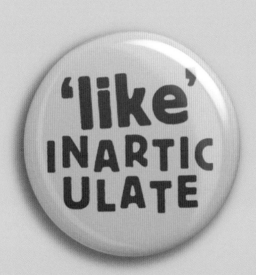

WHO IS THIS BUTTON FOR?

Those utterly preoccupied with one cause—usually of a political nature.[1]

Other monomaniacs.

PROVOCATIVE SUGGESTIONS

Express the deepest regret that you have but one life to sacrifice for your cause.

Ignore the bored facial expressions whenever you bring up your beloved subject.

---

1 The term "single issue fanatic" was coined by the British journalist and writer, Bernard Levin.

WHO IS THIS BUTTON FOR?

Those taking full responsibility in these times of challenging meteorological conditions.

Cyclists and recyclists.

People who voluntarily calculate and pay for their own carbon footprints.

XR[1] activists.

PROVOCATIVE SUGGESTIONS

Be super proud to be politically correct on the most PC issue of our time.

Spend at least one hour every day arguing online with global warming skeptics and agnostics.

Inform all your frequent-flyer friends that just one plane trip undoes a whole year of household recycling.

Mother Earth literally needs people like you—don't let her down!

1   Extinction Rebellion

WHO IS THIS BUTTON FOR?

The bullied, who still manage to hold their heads high.

People who bravely endure unfair criticism.

Other martyrs.

PROVOCATIVE SUGGESTIONS

Share your woes on TV shows, talk radio, and of course, social media.

Litigate to vindicate, not compensate.

Class action suits are a fine way to meet like-minded friends.

WHO IS THIS BUTTON FOR?

Perseverers, strivers, and other indefatigable persisters.

Sisyphus.[1]

PROVOCATIVE SUGGESTIONS

Never, ever, ever, ever, ever, ever give up!

Dogged determination is as important as getting results. Well, almost.

---

1   In Greek mythology, Sisyphus was a king whom the gods punished for deceitfulness by compelling him to roll an immense boulder up a hill, only to watch it roll back down as it neared the top—and to repeat this for eternity.

Why not?

WHO IS THIS BUTTON FOR?

You, when all your subselves are quiet.

PROVOCATIVE SUGGESTIONS

If you feel compelled to provoke the emergence of this voice in others, do so *with affection in the heart and a twinkle in the eye.*[1]

Don't worry, your heightened state of consciousness won't last long.

---

1   Frank Farrelly's Golden Rule of Provocative Therapy.

WHO IS THIS BUTTON FOR?

Yes, but... technicians.

Anyone else who says "Yes, but..." a lot.

Other conflicted people.

PROVOCATIVE SUGGESTIONS

Yes, but what if ____?

Try saying "Yes, and..." instead of "Yes, but..." [1]

---

1   Yes, I know it's difficult to do, but...

Yes, but…you may be saying to yourself.

Yes, they've got a point… **but** surely this is no more than the latest fad in the wacky world of Pop Psychology?

Humor and reverse psychology have been used to provoke people to change their lives for thousands of years. Aristophanes was writing provocative, life-changing, comic plays such as *The Clouds* and *Lysistrata* around 400 BC. Kings and queens employed court jesters to provoke them to make better decisions. The finest comedians not only make us laugh at ourselves and at our society but can also provoke us to change our lives for the better.

Provoked by reverse psychology to see the funny side of a problem, we face the challenge of that problem in a new way. We are liberated and empowered to identify and enact new patterns of behavior for ourselves. When we prescribe our own remedies like this, we are much more likely to take them. We are the only ones who know exactly how we should change our lives. By compassionately laughing at our foibles, addictions, and bad habits, we give ourselves a chance to behave differently and be happy—instead of only almost happy.

If I am not for myself, who will be for me?
And if I am only for myself, what am I?
And if not now, when?

—Hillel the Elder

ACKNOWLEDGMENTS

Frank Farrelly, the founder of Provocative Therapy and my teacher and supervisor, the extraordinary Joe Berke, were always in my mind when creating this book.

Hal and Sidra Stone's concept of Voice Dialogue and John Rowan's writing on subpersonalities were important in helping us design badges that use satire to quieten the parts of people's personalities that have become too loud for their own good.

All my patients who inspired me with their positive reactions to clinical reverse psychology and warmhearted humor in the consulting room and helped me keep going on this project for so many years. As did all my friends (you know who you are) who helped, laughed, encouraged, or even just asked how the book was going. The sagelike advice of my colleague and close friend of over forty years, Stephen Miller, MD, throughout this project, was invaluable. Richard Joseph has championed this book for many years and it was an absolute pleasure working with his splendid son Jack at *Loba*.

My close friend Arnold Brown, the grandfather of stand up comedy in the UK, has always supported the *Almost Happy* project and helped in many ways. The world class improvisational actors Neil Mullarkey and Lee Simpson were there for me when I needed their inspiration.

As far as getting some very necessary Provocative Therapy and coaching for myself, I have always been able to turn to my talented colleague and friend, Phil Jeremiah IV, who has an uncanny ability to make me laugh at my annoying subselves within minutes!

The buttons could not have been made without the creative and technical expertise of our friends Dana Kidson, Louis Whittal, and Matt Wallach to whom we are very grateful.

The contribution of my beloved wife, Hephzibah, has been central to the creation of this book from the first day it was conceived. Her experience as an artist, art psychotherapist, and experienced psychotherapy supervisor who has trained in Provocative Therapy was vital and her love, encouragement, and unpaid therapy on me helped me see this book through to the end. Our son, Jonah, has lived much of his life in parallel to *Almost Happy* and helped in many ways, but a few particularly poignant and kind words he said to me at a tough time in the process will stay with me forever.

—**Brian**

Art, comedy, and therapy have blended into a lifelong triple decker journey. So many professional influences and influencers, teachers, clients, friends, and lived experiences have enriched the themes in this book. *Almost Happy* truly is an amalgamation of many creative minds, psychological attitudes, and comedic perspectives.

Special thanks to: Joe Berke, an extraordinary psychiatrist with whom I worked for six years; Frank Farrelly, who stayed with us for six provocative days; my colleagues at London Art Therapy Centre who help keep the creative dialogue ongoing; Georgi, Bart and the challenging funny friends who call me to account when needed; and all the subversive thinkers and artists who have shared their views on *Almost Happy*.

My creative, authorial, and loving partnership with Brian is a constant source of nourishment and inspiration. You taught me to write— thank you. Our son, Jonah, keeps us both on track, and I have learnt much from his astute yet gentle disposition. Finally, as the "Wife of Brian", I echo thanks to everyone in his acknowledgments too.

—Hephzibah

APPENDICES

APPENDIX I

THE GOALS OF PROVOCATIVE THERAPY

The aim of Provocative Therapy is to change people's behavior for the better. Frank Farrelly outlined five essential goals of Provocative Therapy. The process aims to provoke the clients to:

a. *Affirm their self-worth, both verbally and behaviorally.*

b. *Assert themselves appropriately both in task performance and relationships.*

c. *Defend themselves realistically and authentically against the excessively negative assessments others make of them.*

d. *Engage in psychosocial reality testing and learning the necessary discriminations to respond adaptively: global perceptions lead to global reactions; differentiated perceptions lead to adaptive reactions.*

e. *Engage in risk-taking behaviors in personal relationships, especially communicating affection and vulnerability to significant others.*[1]

---

1 Frank Farrelly and Jeff Brandsma. *Provocative Therapy.* Cupertino, CA: Meta Publications, Inc. 1974 (p. 56).

THE TWO HYPOTHESES OF PROVOCATIVE THERAPY

Frank Farrelly formulated the two central hypotheses of Provocative Therapy as follows:

1. *If provoked by the therapist (humorously, perceptively, and within the client's own internal frame of reference), the client will tend to move in the opposite direction from the therapist's definition of the client as a person.*

2. *If urged provocatively (humorously and perceptively) by the therapist to continue his self-defeating, deviant behaviors, the client will tend to engage in self- and other enhancing behaviors, which more closely approximate the societal norm.[1]*

In other words: People don't like being told what to do. When an obviously kind, insightful, and humorous therapist or life coach advises them to continue doing the very things that are making them unhappy, they tend to disagree with this "advice," stop their inappropriate behavior, and prescribe sensible solutions for themselves.

---

1 Frank Farrelly and Jeff Brandsma. *Provocative Therapy.* Cupertino, CA: Meta Publications, Inc. 1974 (p. 52).

APPENDIX II

THE DYNAMIC OF REVERSE PSYCHOLOGY

The buttons and provocative suggestions (or "sujestions") in *Almost Happy* are inspired by the dynamic of reverse psychology. We have called the process by which unhelpful patterns of behavior are interrupted by humor, absurdity, and reverse psychology, *mirrored pattern interruption (mpi).*

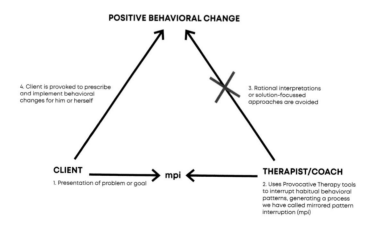

The goal of the process is to provoke the client to engage in more congruent behavior. Thus Provocative Therapy is a form of behavioral therapy and, like Cognitive behavioral therapy (CBT), is pragmatic and focused on stimulating behavioral change. Unlike CBT and some other forms of therapy, it eschews any sharing of rational analysis with the client and instead employs a number of provocative tools (see Appendix III) to provoke the client indirectly to abandon unhelpful patterns of thought and behavior, allowing the voice of common sense and conscience to emerge.

APPENDIX III

THE TOOLS OF PROVOCATIVE THERAPY

While dozens of provocative tactics are used in the clinic and *Almost Happy* workshops, this table comprises fourteen of the provocative tools most frequently employed by the buttons and suggestions in this book.

1	*Label and categorize the client.*	Giving the client a slightly inane label provokes him/her to free him/herself from that label.
2	*Use nicknames.*	Teasing with less-than-complimentary nicknames provokes the client to defend him/herself and dump the behavior suggested by the nickname.
3	*"What's wrong with that?"*	Questioning the existence of any problem provokes focus on the real issue and possible solutions.
4	*"Do more of the same!"*	Encouraging an escalation of unhealthy habitual behavior provokes the ending of bad habits.
5	*Congratulate the client.*	Complimenting the client on being privileged enough to have *such a problem* provokes a re-evaluation of life issues.

6	*Point out the hidden benefits.*	Enthusing about the secondary gain to be obtained from a problem provokes a reassessment of the issue.
7	*"Everything is in balance and must not be changed."*	Warning clients of the danger of abandoning their necessary roles in the world provokes healthy risk-taking for self-improvement.
8	*Play the blame game.*	Encouraging clients to blame everything and everyone for their problems provokes them to take responsibility for their lives.
9	*"There really is no solution to your problem!"*	Conceding that the situation is hopeless and beyond treatment provokes the revelation of appropriate solutions.
10	*Make an absurd suggestion.*	Offering insane solutions to problems provokes the client to come up with more realistic solutions of his/her own.
11	*"This is how the world works!"*	Appealing to the client to accept things as they are provokes meaningful action toward a better life.
12	*Lower your expectations to avoid disappointment.*	Encouraging the client to aim low provokes him/her into setting realistic goals for him/herself.
13	*"Don't rush into anything!"*	Suggesting sensible postponement of any life changes provokes immediate action.
14	*"This is no time to develop a conscience."*	Reminding clients that they can delay resolving moral and ethical dilemmas provokes congruent decision-making.

APPENDIX IV

THEORIES OF SUBSELVES

When we speak of being in "two minds" about something, it does not mean we really have two minds but that we may hold two different positions on something. These views may be held and expressed by different aspects of our selves, or subselves.

The psychological idea that we are composed of different subselves, or different "voices" or subpersonalities, as well as other synonymous terms, has been posited by many psychologists and psychotherapists in modern history. We are indebted to John Rowan for a more comprehensive list from which the examples in the table below were chosen.[1]

YEAR	PSYCHOLOGIST/ PSYCHOTHERAPIST	TERMS USED FOR SUBSELVES OR SUBPERSONALITIES
1923	FREUD	Id Ego Superego
1928	JUNG	Archetypes (e.g., shadow, animus, anima)
1936	LEWIN	Subregions of the personality
1948	KLEIN	Internal objects

1951	PERLS	Top dog Underdog
1961	BERNE	Ego states
1968	BALINT	"The child in the patient" (or inner child)
1970	LEDERMANN	True and false self
1972	STONE, H. & S.	Voice Dialogue Psychology of selves
1970 1973	JANOV LAING	False or unreal self Divided self
1971 1972 1976 1980	O'CONNOR GERGEN SHAPIRO MARTINDALE	Subselves
1974	GOFFMAN	Multiple selfing
1975 1985 1990 1992	ASSAGIOLI REDFEARN ROWAN SLIKER	Subpersonalities
1981	ROGERS, T. B.	Prototypes
1982	BEAHRS	Alter-personalities
1984 2003 2003	KIHISTROM/ ANTOR YOUNG et al. PENNINGTON	Self-schemas
1985	McADAMS	Imagoes
1985	STONE & WINKLEMAN	Energy patterns

1986	WATKINS	Imaginal objects ("imaginary friend")
1986	ORNSTEIN	Small minds
1986	MINSKY	Agents and agencies
1987	MARKUS	Possible selves
1997	HERMANS	I-positions
2000	MEARNS & THORNE	Configurations of self
2007	BOGART	Personas

1 John Rowan. *Discover Your Subpersonalities*. Routledge, 2017.

Dr. Joseph H. Berke (January 17, 1939 – January 11, 2021)
We will miss your jester spirit.